HEROIN

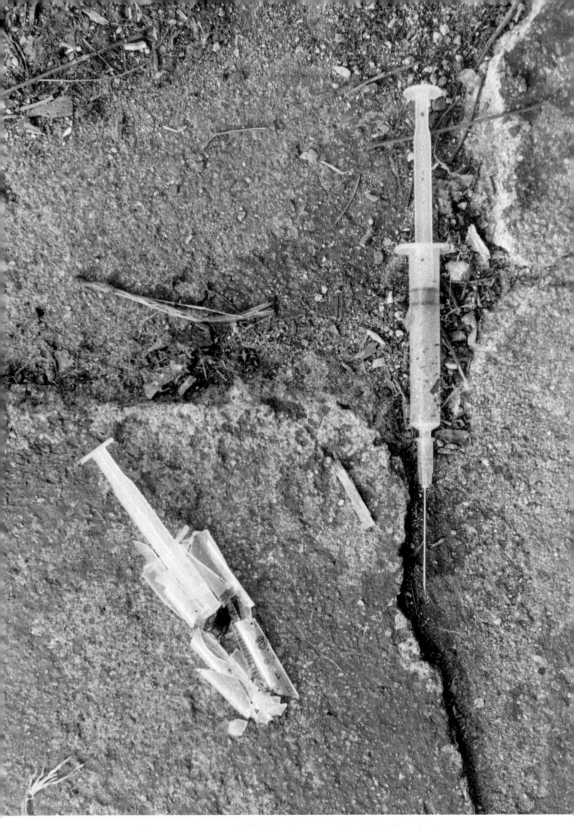

IV-drug users are at high risk of contracting AIDS by sharing needles.

THE DRUG ABUSE PREVENTION LIBRARY

HEROIN

Sandra Lee Smith

THE ROSEN PUBLISHING GROUP, INC.
NEW YORK

To my brother-in-law, Richard,
whose expertise in the prevention of substance abuse
has been invaluable not only to the writing of this book
but to our community.

The people pictured in this book are only models; they, in no way, practice or endorse the activities illustrated. Captions serve only to explain the subjects of photographs and do not in any way imply a connection between the real-life models and the staged situations.

Published in 1991 by The Rosen Publishing Group, Inc.
29 East 21st Street, New York, NY 10010

First Edition

Printed in Canada

Library of Congress Cataloging-in-Publication Data

Smith, Sandra Lee
    Heroin/by Sandra Lee Smith. — 1st ed.
    (The Drug Abuse Prevention Library)
    Includes bibliographical references and index.
    Summary: Discusses heroin, its unique qualities and dangers, and counsels against illegal involvement with the drug.
        ISBN 0-8239-1268-X
        1. Heroin—Juvenile literature. 2. Heroin habit—Juvenile literature. [1. Heroin. 2. Drug Abuse.]
        I. Title II. Series
        HV5809.5.S65 1991
        362.29'3—dc20   91-10676
                                        CIP
                                        AC

Contents

Introduction

*I*magine a high-tech science laboratory. The scientists want to invent and build an advanced robotic machine. They have a special purpose for building this machine, so they invest millions of dollars. They use the money to hire the top scientists in the world. They set up the best-equipped laboratory in existence.

Even though they have all this high-tech equipment, it takes years for them to come up with the perfect machine. They work long hours figuring out formulas. When they find something that they think might work, they spend time and money building a model. When the model is complete, they try out the robot.

Each time a robot is tested, the scientists take note of all the elements that are working properly. Next they list the things that don't work. They then go back to the drawing board and spend millions of dollars ironing out the wrinkles in their design.

More months go by, and new models are developed. Each model is better than the last. Each test brings the scientists closer to their goal. Sometimes setbacks occur and the scientists get discouraged. Sometimes they have to go back a few steps and start over.

Through patience and persistence they continue to experiment with new ideas. They are dedicated in their search for this robot. Their perseverance pays off. One day they try a new model and it works perfectly.

This robot they name Tobor. It does amazing things. Tobor can work complicated problems and compute high-tech data. Tobor moves freely, using limbs similar to those of a human being. Arms and hands enable it to pick up objects. It even has the fine motor coordination to assemble delicate equipment.

The most amazing feature of Tobor is its ability to service itself. If a computer

8 chip fails to work, Tobor can find it and tell the scientists. Some repairs it can make itself. For example, it can oil some of its parts.

Another feature that the scientists are happy about is that Tobor can process information. It can feed programs into its memory bank and enlarge its capacity to function.

Tobor is so complex that it seems almost human. Some of the scientists even think of Tobor as being alive. Not only that, they have become very fond of the robot in a human way.

One day, however, Tobor does an astounding thing. No one was expecting this to happen, so no one was ready for the resulting disaster. Tobor walked over to the chemistry lab and poured a very corrosive chemical into its system.

The scientists panicked. They rushed to the robot and began flushing the parts. Tobor seemed unaffected, but just to be sure, they ran several tests. Tobor was still functioning. With relief, the scientists programmed Tobor's memory bank, instructing the robot to stay away from the chemical.

Somehow the reprogramming did not work. Every day Tobor poured the chemi-

The athlete works hard to develop his body. He chooses not to harm it with drugs.

10 cal into its system. The scientists tried to hide the chemical. But the robot's sensors were always able to pick up traces of the substance and find it.

The scientists were frantic. The repeated exposure to the chemical finally weakened the surface layers of Tobor's computer. It was beginning to damage the robot's parts. System failures began occurring, each one more severe than the last.

The scientists had to stand by and watch their beautiful machine continue its process of self-destruction. There was nothing they could do as they saw all the time and money disappearing before their eyes. Each day another function dissolved under the destructive chemical. Each day the scientists' spirits dropped another notch. It was such a waste.

You might think that an invention as great as that robot should not destroy itself. How stupid! How wasteful! Yet humans do that to themselves every time they put a chemical substance into their bodies.

In a way, our bodies are like the robotic machine. We are built to move around, to think, and to operate complicated functions. Not only can our minds and bodies accomplish marvelous feats, but they can fuel themselves and heal breakdowns or injuries.

We are a miracle of creation, and we all have a special purpose. Each one of us is unique and designed for individual accomplishments. Because of our free will and self-determination, we can operate in our own way. It is impossible, however, to accomplish your purpose or to function properly if you do as Tobor did and pour corrosive chemicals into your body.

Heroin is a chemical that destroys the body and the mind. At first the body has enough strength and resilience to resist the poison. Repeated exposure weakens the system, however, and some day your body will begin to self-destruct just as surely as Tobor's did.

Think how valuable you are as a human being. There is no other being created like you or for your purpose. Your body and mind need full power and capacity to fulfill that purpose. It is your responsibility to see that they are maintained in working order.

Poppies are beautiful flowers, but they yield a deadly substance.

CHAPTER 1

What Is Heroin?

*H*eroin is a chemical substance derived from the opium poppy. This beautiful flower grows in hot, dry climates. The pod left after the petals fall contains a white syrup that is collected by poppy growers. When the syrup dries, it hardens into a brown substance we call opium.

From opium, chemists extract many of our common drugs. Some of those drugs are used legally for medicinal purposes. Morphine and codeine are the most common ones. They are widely used by doctors as painkillers.

14   Heroin is also a common derivative, but it is illegal in most countries, including the United States. It is considered so harmful and dangerous that it is not even allowed to be used for medicinal purposes. Mainly that is because it is made from the garbage left over after making morphine.

That was not always the case. During the mid-nineteenth century a famous German chemist made heroin to help morphine addicts come off the drug. Morphine was widely used at the time as a painkiller.

The drug was considered a *heroic* substance. Soldiers from the Civil War up to World War I were given heroin to break them of their addiction to morphine. It was after the turn of the century that doctors began to realize that heroin addiction was far worse than morphine.

Now scientists have developed another chemical to assist the heroin addict. Methadone is used by some drug treatment centers throughout the United States to help heroin addicts withdraw. There is concern, however, that methadone is also addictive. In fact, some studies indicate that it is as addictive as heroin.

Manufacture of Heroin

It is illegal to grow opium poppies in the United States. Even if we could grow them, a laboratory is needed to process the syrup into the powders sold on the street. Such labs are also illegal.

Most of the international supply of opium comes from poppy farms in two major areas: the Golden Crescent and the Golden Triangle. Poppy farms and factories are illegal in those areas also. But the people are so poor that they risk punishment to grow the flowers.

The Golden Crescent is in the Middle East and includes the countries of Iran, Afghanistan, and Pakistan. The Golden Triangle is in South Asia and includes Laos, Burma, and Thailand. All of these countries are very poor. A farmer can early 97 percent more money from a crop of poppies than from the same amount of grain.

Most of these countries are engaged in wars. Because of that, police action is focused on warfare, leaving little time and money to fight drug trafficking. Also, these countries need expensive weapons. Drugs are often exchanged for arms.

16   In the western United States heroin is imported from Mexico. *Mexican Brown* is a poorly processed grade of heroin made from poppies grown south of the border. It is of very low quality, but the demand for it is so high that the makers see no need to spend money to process a better quality.

These social and economic conditions make it difficult to control the production of opium poppies. As long as people will buy their product, these poor countries will produce opium.

Transporting opium to the United States is illegal. However, opium slips through customs in many ways. Because of the increased attention of law-enforcement agencies, the drug scene on the streets is changing. Shipments of marijuana, which is strong smelling and bulky, are decreasing while opium and cocaine importation is increasing. The more compact substances are easier to smuggle into the country.

Unfortunately, the demand for all these drugs is high. Dealing them on the black market and on the street involves millions of dollars. The power of that much money makes it very hard to control the various

Drug-sniffing dogs help law-enforcement officers to check
luggage at airports.

18 sellers, dealers, and buyers. From the drug barons to the street dealers to the neighborhood pushers to the users themselves, greed and need rule supply and demand.

Because the market is illegal, it is not regulated. That leaves the business wide open to corruption, danger, and death. From the start of the chain in the Middle East and Southeast Asia, dirty laboratories begin the potential for death.

Buyers never know what purity or dosage they are getting in the packs of powder they buy. No laws control what is added to the substance. So a user faces not only addiction and the ill effects of the drug, but the possibility of overdose or poisoning or both.

Dealing the drugs is also dangerous. Heroin is illegal, so whatever level of the business you are involved in is criminal. Criminal activity not only is immoral but involves the dealer with immoral people. Those people are likely to cheat, steal, lie, and even kill. That happens at all levels, from the baron protecting his turf to the addicts who are so desperate for an injection that they kill for it.

You may think you are safe because
friends or family supply your needs. But
somewhere in your dealing you will come
across a possibly life-threatening situation.
It could be the quality of the heroin or the
person you deal with.

Other Names for Heroin

The big H	Scag
H	Stuff
Smack	Elephant
Chi	Tiger
Dragon	Nanoo
No. 4	Gear
No. 3	China White
Harry	Black Tar
Junk	Chiva
Scat	Mexican Brown
Horse	Tar
Chinese	Mexican Tar

A heroin addict shoots up—injects heroin to get one of many fixes in a day.

CHAPTER 2

How Does Heroin Make You Feel?

*H*eroin is a narcotic. The word narcotic comes from the Greek word *narkosis,* which means benumbed. Physically, heroin numbs the senses.

Physical Effects

Our five senses enable us to survive in our environment. Taste, smell, touch, hearing, and sight feed messages to our brain so that we can react to what is around us. If we don't like what is around us, we have choices. We can change the environment, move to a new location, or ignore what is there. Most of us learn to function within the circumstances.

21

22 As teenagers it is not always possible to make changes. The choice to ignore is difficult, especially if the environment is depressing, lonely, or ugly. The addict's wish is to escape. Chemical substances deaden the senses and let one ignore the surroundings.

The problem with that form of escape is that whatever makes you want to escape doesn't change. Drugs wear off and there you are, still facing the same problems.

Heroin not only deadens your senses, it becomes physically addicting. After long use it stops giving you a high, yet it is very painful to withdraw from use.

The first-time user of heroin often becomes violently ill, with vomiting and severe headache. Peers or pushers say it is better the second time. For some, it isn't.

Most people do get a rush or a buzz the first few minutes after smoking or injecting heroin. Each time you use it, though, you need a larger dose to get the same feeling. After continual use that rush no longer happens, but by then you are addicted.

Heroin is used in several ways. The most common way is smoking. Some swallow it, but that is rarely effective.

Because of the tolerance that builds up, *23*
users switch from smoking to injecting the
heroin directly into the blood. The rush is
immediate and stronger.

When you use heroin, your body builds
up a resistance to it. In order to get a
high, you need more of the drug each
time. Another alternative is to *skin-pop.*
By injecting the drug under the skin, not
in a vein, the high comes quicker than by
smoking it.

Skin popping soon becomes ineffective,
and the addict needs to *mainline* the injection into the vein. Heroin, however, makes
veins collapse, so a long-time user has to
find new veins to inject. That gives the
junkie the tracks you hear about, especially if dirty needles are used.

If you are allergic to heroin or any opi-
ate, you can become violently ill and even
die on the first fix. Heroin that has been
made and handled poorly, is not mea-
sured, or is mixed with poison can cause
overdose or death. There is no way of
knowing when or if that will happen.

An overdose can cause heart failure,
rapid heartbeat, shortness of breath, and
ringing in the ears or head. Some heroin
overdoses cause coma, or unconscious-

24 ness. That is extremely dangerous, as victims can fall and smother or drown in their own vomit.

Continual use of heroin causes extreme constipation and a loss of appetite. Many addicts suffer from malnutrition for one of two reasons: First, they are not hungry. Second, and more commonly, the constipation becomes so painful that they don't want to eat more food.

Emotional Effects

Most people get to heroin because they have been doing other drugs. As we have suggested, use of chemical substances is a form of escape. It is an emotional reaction to one's life situation. Instead of dealing with life, users choose to escape it.

Another emotional aspect of addiction to heroin and other substances is the *rip and run* thrill. Teenagers who do not see themselves as successful or do not see life as meaningful make a world for themselves that is filled with a series of daily purposes and successes.

The actual drug is not the purpose. It is the whole process of finding the stuff, getting the money for it, scoring the hit, and then riding the high. They are not

Counselors can help teens find a way out of the misery of drug addiction.

taking drugs, but *doing* drugs. Their day is a whole series of small, yet significant successes.

This false sense of purpose and accomplishment often replaces a teenager's view that life lacks real purpose and accomplishment.

Everyone can find meaning and purpose in life. They can do so by searching within and finding and working toward goals. Choosing the escape of drugs leads to the same process that Tobor went through. Repeated use of heroin or any chemical substance corrodes the brain, the organs, and the body. This route is a sure journey to death. Searching within and acting upon your values and goals is a road to life.

Running away from home makes many teenagers easy prey for
drug pushers and pimps.

CHAPTER 3

How Do You Get Heroin?

*C*ontrary to the common myth, heroin is easy to get. You don't always have to deal with a hardened criminal on the street. Most teens get their smack from someone they know.

Drug dealers try to work through a network of high school students for two reasons: it protects them from getting caught, and it makes it easier to move the drugs. They target popular figures such as sports heroes and leaders. Their purpose is to make *doing* drugs the "in" thing. It usually works.

The outside dealers are usually the gangs and pushers who get the heroin

28 from the border to the neighborhood. Because of the money involved, dealers and pushers do not operate within the law. They don't have to because their activities are already illegal. They lie, cheat, steal from one another, and sometimes murder.

These are the people who *handle* the heroin you buy. They are the ones who mix the concentrated heroin with other powders such as flour, sugar, chalk, baking soda, rat poison, and strychnine.

Keep in mind that they do not follow any standards. They are not under codes or rules. Therefore you have no way of knowing what the heroin has been mixed or *cut* with nor how strong it is. That is how overdoses occur.

The dealers and pushers are interested only in their own profit and protection. They have no concern for you, the consumer.

Friends

Friends don't care what they sell. Often they buy cheaper heroin, a poor quality mixed with more powder. They sell that to you and keep the better stuff for themselves.

When you buy heroin on the street you could be buying anything.

Many drug pushers in school sell to pay for their own habit. They "do" their profit. For example, they buy an eighth-of-an-ounce packet, or what they call an *eight ball*. They take some out for themselves and then *step on it*. That is a slang term meaning to add a powder to it to make it an eighth of an ounce again. Then they sell it as an eight ball. By the time you purchase a fix from a friend, it may be diluted or dangerously mixed with counteracting powders.

The pushers target popular students at school. Many of the students' friends don't

30 even know that they do the big H. They use their popularity to find a market for their supply. They don't care what happens to the students who buy their goods as long as they make enough profit to pay for their own.

Pushers/Dealers

Most of you are probably saying to yourselves, "I'd never get mixed up with a hardcore pusher or a gang member." Most students don't. They buy from friends, and some even get their supply from family members. That is how drug dealers operate. They develop a network of suppliers within the school. They target popular figures to create a false sense of security. As we have pointed out, most of those students sell to support their own habit.

Drug dealers or pushers often offer free hits to possible runners. They give free smack until the targets are hooked. Then when they have to start buying their own stuff, the pusher tells them to sell some and take their junk from the profits.

Some dealers offer free heroin to female students until they are hooked. Then they force the girls to prostitute themselves for their supply. The dealers usually use the girls themselves at first. When they tire of the girls they start them on a career in the streets.

Through this process, the dealers insure that they have a market and a network in which to move the market. Most gang members do not use drugs themselves. They see the results and don't want to destroy themselves. All they want is profit. They have no concern for you personally. All you are to them is supply and demand.

Family

Unfortunately, many young people get drugs from family members. They often believe that they can trust such a supply. That is false security. The family member has to purchase the stuff from the same dealers the students at school do. It may not be the same person, but the heroin has traveled through the same unsavory chan-nels.

The fact that heroin is illegal in this country and is not even allowed for medi-cal purposes doubles its danger. Using even the cleanest heroin destroys your body, but unmeasured, unclean heroin can do so faster.

When parents drink and smoke, the stage is set for their teenagers to experiment with drugs.

CHAPTER 4

Why Do People Use Drugs?

The largest population of substance abusers and addicts is the adult community. Therefore it should not surprise us to learn that most teenagers learn to do drugs from their parents.

All through childhood the cure for a problem is a pill. We see our parents have a drink to relax, to unwind, to party, and to escape. Many teenagers have seen their parents smoke marijuana or do cocaine or heroin or both.

Children copy their parents. That is the way it has been throughout the centuries. The drugs may not be the same, but the behavior of taking a substance to cure, forget, or tolerate a problem is.

34   If Mom and Dad have a couple of drinks to feel good at a party, why can't you do the same? Or even better, do a stronger drug? Smoking marijuana, snorting cocaine, hitting on smack, aren't you doing the same as they are when they have several drinks?

It is hard to tell the difference, except that alcohol is a legal drug. What needs to be looked at is why adults or teenagers need to do drugs at all. Often we need to help our parents break substance-abuse habits as much as we need to break them ourselves.

Curiosity

Some teens do drugs because they want to know what it feels like. Many try heroin for the same reason. If pot or coke is good, they think, the big H must be even better.

Along with curiosity is the element of risk: the dares from peers, the challenge of trying something new, the element of danger. That is a false sense of adventure.

The risk may not seem high when peers or family members have already done the big H. But each use has possible danger. There are better ways to satisfy your curiosity, be challenged, or face changes.

Resisting drugs could actually be a **35**
bigger challenge. The appeal of drugs is
that escaping a problem through them is
easier and requires less energy than fight-
ing the problem. Many who say the big H
is a challenge really are afraid to accept
the true challenge of saying no.

Peer Pressure

If you are doing something that you
know is wrong but you want to keep on
doing it, you have an inner conflict. That
usually results in guilt. To get rid of that
feeling of guilt, it is normal to try to justify
your actions.

Students who enjoy doing drugs often
try to talk their friends into doing it because that makes their behavior seem
acceptable. They can square it with themselves: "If everyone is doing the big H, it
must be okay."

Peers who try to pressure you into taking heroin are not doing you a favor. They
may be trying to get you to do it so that
they can believe they are okay. As we have
already seen, others may pressure you
because they are trying to pay for their
own habit.

Developing a strong sense of self-worth
protects you from giving in to peer pressure.

36 Setting goals gives you a larger view to be able to make decisions that will be for your own good, not someone else's.

Stilling the Sense of Lack

Most teenage addicts say that their feelings of not being good enough are the major reason for doing drugs. Some feel that their families don't love them. If you think your parents are happiest when you're out of their hair, that causes a sense of being unwanted.

Unfortunately, parents get so caught up in the struggle to earn a living that it may seem they don't love you. Heroin will not fill that lack. It deadens the sense of loss but never substitutes for the real thing.

There are many ways to find people who will care about you. The best way to get people to love you and care about you is to love and care for someone else. Many other teenagers feel as lost as you do. Old people are lonely in your neighborhood. Little children, latchkey kids, are alone and in danger from the drug scene too.

You can decide to deaden your feeling of need or fill it. Helping other lost people fills that sense of being unloved or not needed. Your family may not have time for you, but someone does need you.

Living up to your responsibilities helps to create a positive self-image.

38   Other teenagers may have family love but think their peers do not respect them. Doing drugs does not buy respect. You have seen that student pushers are under pressure to build a market to sell their drugs or to give belief to their lie that doing drugs is okay.

Other teenagers feel the way you do. Find out who they are and together build relationships that give you friends without drugs.

After-school activities, school clubs, community centers, and religious groups have programs through which you can help others in enjoyable projects.

Your life may be difficult. Your family may not be what you want it to be. You may not have the friends you think you should have. No situations are ever perfect. Every person at one time or another feels a sense of need. Every person at one time or another feels that there is no purpose in life.

The difference among us is how we react to those conditions. We always have freedom to choose how to handle the situation. We can choose to run and hide. We can choose to blame everyone else. We can choose heroin or other drugs.

In an outpatient rehabilitation center, teenage heroin addicts receive daily doses of methadone as replacement therapy.

The point is that it *is* our choice. We can always choose to face our life as it is. We can change it. The only way to do that is with clear thinking.

There is no condition in this world that has not been faced by another human being. There is no condition that we cannot get out of. No one controls our will.

No matter how bad the circumstances seem, there is always somewhere to go, someone to help, and some way to climb out of it. Choosing drugs is one way. Choosing life is another.

Many teenagers lose friends to death from heroin overdose.

What Kind of Trouble Will Heroin Bring?

*H*eroin is not quite as swiftly dangerous as some people think. It numbs the brain and slowly corrodes the internal system. Yet many people do survive for years with daily use. Unfortunately, taking heroin regularly is addictive.

The definition of addiction is giving yourself over to something that becomes a habit. In other words, you enslave yourself to heroin. Instead of your controlling your own life, your life is controlled by the need for the big H. Taking heroin is selling yourself into slavery.

42 *Health*

Heroin is more damaging to mental health than to physical health. Addiction is psychological dependency. It leads to depression and often to suicide.

Think of the stories of humiliation and debilitation that slaves suffered in the past. Present-day heroin addicts are no different. They are often forced into prostitution, illegal drug-running, crime, and murder. That is partly because of the people they associate with. But it is also because doing heroin every day is very expensive. Most people addicted to heroin have trouble holding a job. They cannot concentrate on work, nor can they keep regular hours.

More dangerous than that, however, is the loss of self-worth one feels after committing crimes. Most heroin addicts need to deal with psychological problems as much as physical ones.

The dangers to the body include the risk of convulsive shock. Because of the way heroin is produced and marketed, there is a big risk of overdose or convulsions because of a bad mixture.

Have you ever seen someone in convulsions when overdosing? It is a frightening sight. The body may may twitch so strongly that the person travels across the room jerking and gyrating. The person has no control of body functions and makes strange and ugly sounds.

Mucus pours out of the eyes and nose. The person drools or, worse, vomits. Lacking motor coordination, he or she may not spit the vomit out, causing himself to drown in it. He or she may urinate and defecate all over himself.

Prompt first aid may pull a person out of this condition. However, he or she may go into a coma for weeks, months, or years. Sometimes the experience damages part of the brain, disabling the person. Is the high from heroin worth that risk?

You might see friends or family smoke or inject heroin and, when nothing bad happens, think it is safe for you. You might be in a *shooting gallery* or place where people go for a fix and see your friends getting high with no problems. Keep in mind that all bodies react differently.

In reality, the biggest health danger from doing heroin are the indirect effects. More dangerous than the actual drug are the diseases you are exposed to. Most of

44 those diseases come from unsanitary injections. AIDS (acquired immune deficiency syndrome), hepatitis B, and blood poisoning (septicemia) are passed through unsterile needles.

Often junkies *backwash* their needles. They inject the heroin, draw some of their own blood to rinse the syringe, then reinject it. They do so to get every bit of heroin. That contact with blood is the main cause of the passing on of diseases.

You may think that you would never use an unsterile needle or *rig*. But many teens find out too late that the needle may have been washed, but washing is not sterilizing. The fact is that sterile needles are harder to get than heroin.

Other side effects are venereal diseases from unprotected sex while on heroin. Taking the big H while pregnant results in addicted babies. Continual use of smack damages the reproductive organs and causes infertility.

Heroin affects the mind and twists reality. That can cause people to overdose accidentally. It can also cause such severe depression that a person commits suicide. Remember that heroin does not solve the problem. It only hides it for a little while.

Family   45

Family relationships suffer when members are on heroin. Users tend to withdraw into themselves. Communication breaks down, and relationships fall apart. Some families practice "Tough Love" and kick

Loneliness and depression are frequent companions of drug addicts.

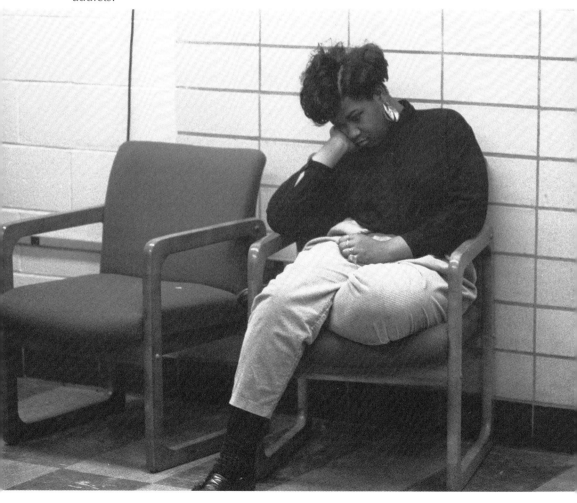

you out of the home until you are off drugs.

Most of these problems happen because of misunderstandings and fear. If you or any of your family show signs of withdrawing, it is important to seek family counseling. You need the emotional support of loved ones. They need to understand what you are going through.

Law

Heroin is an illegal narcotic. Possession or sale is a felony crime. Felony convictions result in hard time in prison.

First-time offenders caught using heroin for reasons not connected with other crimes such as selling, prostitution, or theft may be offered a diversion program. In such a program some states give teenagers the option of volunteering at their own expense to get: (1) counseling; (2) drug prevention education; and (3) periodic urinalysis. If they go through this program successfully, the charges can be dropped.

Not all states have this option. Nor do you have the choice if you are caught a second time. In such cases you are charged as a criminal.

Persons caught possessing heroin for sale or selling the drug are charged with a higher class of felony. The penalties vary from state to state. In many states it is also a crime to have drug equipment such as syringes and pipes.

Another danger facing the user regarding the law is that once you are arrested, or *popped,* you will no longer be trusted by your *junkie* friends. They will think you are working with the police to turn them in. Most teenagers who have been arrested have a hard time scoring a hit.

Another danger is even more serious. Because they are afraid you might snitch, they may give you a *hot shot.* That is an overdose of the big H or a dose laced with poison to kill you.

Death

The final result of doing heroin is death. Everything you do, every decision you make, and every habit you repeat decides the quality of your life.

Life with heroin is not quality living. It is enslavement, disease, and decay. You are too valuable a human being to let heroin control your life.

Positive activities with positive people are a good defense
against the temptation to do drugs.

CHAPTER 6

Where to Go for Help

Many people who take drugs think that their situation is hopeless. That is not true. No situation is ever hopeless. Remember that heroin changes your brain. You may think your condition is worse than it really is.

Addiction is difficult, but *withdrawal is possible*. Habits are hard to break, but *behavior can be changed*. Sickness is hard to overcome, but *people are healed*.

Taking the First Step

The first step toward help is admitting that you have a problem. The next step is to be willing to take action. The third step is to

50 find help. The final step is to commit yourself to the path to recovery.

The first two steps involve you. You make your own choices about your quality of life. It may seem that you are trapped in your life, but that is simply not so. You decide how you react to your situation. No one can control your thoughts or your wishes.

No one can force you to take drugs. No one can force you not to. Maybe incidents of control do occur. For example, if you are in a hospital or in jail you may not be able to shoot up on heroin. If you are enslaved or captured by a gang, you may be forced to take drugs. But look back on your actions. Your own choice of behavior put you in those situations.

If you have allowed circumstances to open you to addiction to heroin, you can still choose to get out. Once you face the need and decide to withdraw, there are many places to go for help.

Family, Friends, Religious Groups

The first place to go is to your family. Most drug addiction involves the whole family, either directly or indirectly. If other members of your family are involved in substance abuse, including alcohol, they will need help as much as you do.

Maybe they don't take part in substance abuse. But if they create problems for you through physical or psychological abuse or neglect or misunderstandings, group therapy can help you solve your differences. If your family relationship is healthy, you will need the love and support of family members to pull you through the ordeal.

Sometimes teenagers do not want their family to know they are involved in drugs. There are other choices. Other relatives or close friends can help you. School counselors can suggest help. Family doctors will treat you or refer you to someone who specializes in substance abuse. Many communities offer social services that include teen centers.

One of the best sources of help is a religious organization. Most of the people in such organizations are trained in counseling and have access to community services. For example, Phoenix, Arizona, has an organization called Clergy Against Drugs. These inner-city pastors are trained in assisting young people who want to withdraw from heroin or other substances. Most large cities have Jewish

52 Family Services, listed in the telephone book as a resource for those of the Jewish faith.

What family, friends, and the religious community offer is emotional support as well as financial or therapeutic support. However, heroin is such a powerful addiction that their help will not be enough. Finding professional help is the next step.

Hotlines

Whether your family is in on your decision or you are struggling alone, you will need trained assistance in withdrawing from heroin. Call a local hotline to find what is available in your area and which programs you can afford or qualify for.

Every major television network announces statewide hotline numbers to call for help. They usually follow a "Say No to Drugs" announcement.

The telephone book has listings in the Yellow Pages. Look in the "D" listings for *Drug Abuse Information and Treatment*. Call one of the clinics or centers and tell them what you need. If one is not the right place for you, they can refer you to other numbers.

If there are no drug listings in your area, try the "A" listings for *Alcoholism*.

You can get help without giving your name on an emergency hotline.

These centers work with the drug abuse centers.

The advantage of phoning for information is that you can be helped to some degree without giving any personal information. The volunteer can tell you which

53

54 clinics will treat you confidentially. Also, clinics range from free to over $2,000 per week in cost. Phoning can help you find the place you can afford. Always remember that help is just a phone call away.

Hotline Emergency

The inside cover of the phone book lists emergency hotlines. They usually have the words *drug, emotional, help,* or *hope* in the number. For example, the number in New York is 1-800-622 HELP for the National Institute on Drug Abuse Treatment Referral. In Arizona the number 1-800-475 HOPE is advertised on television. These are important to know if you are with an overdose victim. Call 911 or one of the emergency numbers.

Some states have emergency teams that specialize in overdoses. Arizona has an organization called TERROS. These men and women rush to the scene in plain clothes and treat the victim without involving the police. That can be an important consideration. The sight of uniforms or the sound of sirens can frighten an overdose victim into a heart attack.

Guidance

Every major metropolitan area and most counties have services for withdrawal from drugs. They range from government-funded projects to private hospitals. Religious organizations also provide counseling services.

Remember that substance abuse usually involves hidden causes. If you have been using heroin for any length of time, you will need to repair your thinking as well as heal your body. Good counseling and a relationship with a care group will help you to stay off the drug.

Kicking the habit will also mean changing some of your social habits. You might want to consider a new set of friends. Hanging around friends who are into drugs will be too great a temptation.

Treatment centers can introduce you to new friends who will understand what you are going through and can help you.

Treatment and Rehab Centers

Since withdrawal from heroin "cold turkey" can be painful, many are afraid to quit. That does not have to be the case.

56 Treatment centers offer controlled withdrawal with the help of other substances such as methadon and maltrexone. Some clinics employ acupuncture.

Such treatment enables a person to come off the drug slowly. It also allows him to function at work or school in a normal routine. Withdrawal does not have to be painful.

Unfortunately, many states do not offer methadone to teenagers unless they have failed a twenty-one-day detoxification program.

The programs for teenagers that have been most successful are the rehabilitation centers where they live with other teens coming off the drug.

Helping others is the best way to help yourself. The advantage of living with other addicts is that you can share experiences. There is someone who understands what you are going through.

Rehabilitation centers offer drug abusers a chance to take themselves away from their old environment in a setting that is drug-free. Through counseling and group therapy, they learn ways to rebuild their lives so that they can be free of dependence on heroin or other drugs.

Alcoholic Anonymous and Narcotics Anonymous achieve their success rates by helping their members renew their relationship with family and God. If you belong to a religious organization, or even if you go to a new one where your past is not known, you will be strengthened.

So much of the battle with substance abuse is an inner struggle. Much of the appeal of any drug is emotional and mental. You want peace, freedom from stress, and a sense of well-being.

These can be found on a permanent basis, but not through drugs. Get in touch with your inner self, and strength will come to help you battle the temptation offered by drugs. Find a true and spiritual relationship, and you will find peace, security, well-being, and love.

57

Glossary

Explaining New Words

addiction Inability to resist the urge for a drug.

alternative Choice between two or more courses of action.

cold turkey Quitting the use of a drug without any help.

comatose State of being unconscious, caused by disease, injury, or poison.

constipation Difficult passage of hard, dry feces.

corrosive Gradually eating away, like rust.

cut To mix heroin with a powder.

derivative Made from another material.

eight ball Eighth of an ounce packet.

emulate To try to be like someone.

felony Serious crime that results in severe punishment.

hot shot Overdose of heroin, or a dose laced with poison designed to kill the user.

injection Placing of a substance directly into the blood, usually with a needle.

junkie Person addicted to drugs.

laboratory Place where scientists work.

mainline To inject heroin directly into the blood through a vein.

malnutrition Poor health caused by not eating an adequate diet.

popped Arrested.

prosecute To charge in court with a crime.

prostitute Person who is paid for performing sexual acts.

rehabilitation Restoring to former health, or putting back into good condition.

rig The needle and tourniquet used to inject heroin.

rip and run Process of doing drugs in which you *rip* or get the drug and then *run* to find more.

robotics Science of making robots.

scoring a hit Buying heroin.

shooting gallery Place where people gather to get shots of heroin.

skin pop To inject heroin under the skin, not directly into the vein.

step on it Slang term for taking some heroin out of a packet and adding powder to refill the packet.

Help List

- American Council for Drug Education
  204 Monroe Street
  Rockville, MD 20852
  (301) 294-0600

- National Clearinghouse for Alcohol and
      Drug Information
  P.O Box 2345
  Rockville, MD 20852
  (301) 468-2600

- Narcotics Anonymous
  World Service Office
  16155 Wyandotte Street
  Van Nuys, CA 91406

- National Federation of Parents for
      Drug-Free Youth
  8730 Georgia Avenue
  Silver Spring, MD 20910
  1-800-554-KIDS (5437)

- NIDA Clearinghouse for Drug
      Information
  P.O Box 416
  Kensington, MD 20795

For Further Reading

Ball, Jacqueline. *Everything You Need to Know About Drug Abuse.* New York: Rosen Publishing Group, 1990.

Edwards, Gabrielle. *Coping with Drug Abuse.* New York: Rosen Publishing Group, 1990.

Godfrey, Martin. *Heroin.* New York: Franklin Watts, 1987.

Jackson, Michael and Brude. *Doing Drugs.* New York: St. Martin's Press, 1983.

Kaplan, Leslie. *Coping with Peer Pressure.* New York: Rosen Publishing Group, 1990.

Kurland, Morton. *Coping with AIDS: Facts and Fears.* New York: Rosen Publishing Group, 1990.

62 Lee, Essie E. *Breaking the Connection.*
New York: Julian Messner, 1988.

McFarland, Rhoda. *Coping with Substance Abuse.* New York: Rosen Publishing Group, 1990.

Morgan, H. Wayne. *Drugs in America.* New York: Syracuse University Press, 1981.

Smith, Sandra Lee. *Coping with Decision-Making.* New York: Rosen Publishing Group, 1989.

————. *Value of Self-Control.* New York: Rosen Publishing Group, 1990.

————. *Coping through Self-Control.* New York: Rosen Publishing Group, 1991.

Sunshine, Linda; Wright, John. *The 100 Best Treatment Centers for Alcoholism and Drug Abuse.* New York: Avon Books, 1988.

Toma, David; Levey, Irv. *Toma Tells It Straight with Love.* New York: Bantam, Doubleday, Dell, 1981.

Index

63

About the Author

For twenty-one years, Sandra Lee Smith has taught grades from kindergarten through college level in California and Arizona.

Active on legislative committees and in community projects, she has helped design programs to involve parents in the education process.

In response to the President's Report, *A Nation at Risk,* Ms. Smith participated in a project involving Arizona State University, Phoenix Elementary School District, and an inner-city community in Phoenix. Participants in the project developed a holistic approach to education.

Photo Credits

Cover photo: Chuck Peterson
Photos on pages 2, 9, 25, 29, 32, 37, 40, 45, 48, 59: Chris Volpe; page 13: Gamma Liaison/Dr. Allan W. King; page 17: Gamma Liaison/Roger M. Richards; page 20: Chuck Peterson/Blackbirch Graphics; page 26: Gamma Liaison/James Metropole; page 39: Wide World.

Design and Production: Blackbirch Graphics, Inc.